AF243940

SPICE & BOON

First Published in South Africa 2018

Published by SPICE & BOON Pty (Ltd)

South Africa.

© Afari 2018

ISBN: 978 0 620 78456 6

Cover Design: SPICE & BOON Pty (Ltd)

No text contained within this book was written to mock, ridicule or discredit anyone of their belief(s). This book is written solely to inspire, enlighten and furthermore entertain.

A GARDEN *of* WORDS

AFARI

Contents

A picture may be worth a thousand words, but words can create a thousand pictures more. Words, I love words. More than just creating pictures and tickling our imagination, words define who we really are. Words unite us and they can also cause a divide amongst people. The poetry I have carefully written in this lovely and beautiful book may not satisfy your needs now, but eventually at some point in your life I sincerely hope through reading these words you find the peace and wisdom you're searching for. I wish you all the best in your journey of self-discovery, recovery, and the continuation of building yourself. I hope this book helps you heal, and grow to become the person you strive to be – the best version of yourself.

for the heart

To measure how deeply a person can love,

first gather all the pieces to their **broken** heart.

~ Afari

PROMISE NOTE

I cross my heart

I hope to die,

I swear to never make you cry.

Come rain, come storm;

my love will never change form.

In joy, in pain

my love will remain the same.

Today and *tomorrow*

my heart is here for you to borrow.

But first, take my hand and let's fly;

allow our hearts to float the sky.

I was just a clueless foreigner to what love
was until I found refuge inside your heart.

~ Afari

She was just like the clouds hanging from

the blue sky.

She was close enough for me to see her

but far enough to be touched.

So, all I could do was just **admire** from

a distance.

~ *Afari*

Their lips were home to **different languages** but their hearts were a home with a common language they could both speak fluently; a love language.

~ Afari

GOOD GIRL, BAD BOY.

How could I bring a girl like her into a life like mine?

A world so cold, dark and twisted.

Girls like her have no place in a world like mine.

If she truly knew about me she would keep

her distance.

How could such a bad boy like me become part of an

innocent girl's life?

My presence in her world can yield nothing but

pain and **misery.**

Perhaps if I truly care about her I must let her go.

I'd rather be a man with no heart

than to be a man without soul.

Love comes in many different forms but

your love was the one that **hurt** me the most.

~ *Afari*

Home isn't home without you

and when you left me, love soon

became a language my heart

forgot how to speak.

~ *Afari*

You made me feel something I never thought I would.

My heart was stubborn and my mind was **misunderstood**

Yet, you made me believe in love when no one else could.

~ Afari

You are as **wild** as the waves of the

Ocean and I'm the person standing at the

shoreline afraid of your waves.

~ *Afari*

SINKING

When you left, it felt like I fell into the ocean

 backwards, with my eyes facing the sky.

When I was still floating at the surface

your absence troubled my heart.

I felt alone.

When I was halfway from reaching the

bottom your absence began to matter less.

I wasn't scared of being alone anymore.

When my back hit against the sand, deep

within the ocean's bottom;

I got used to the pain.

When the **sinking** was over I learnt

how to smile again and this time it was without you.

Don't let the desires of your heart blind
you from seeing that which you have
already been **blessed** with.

~ *Afari*

"I love you" should have meant something to you

because it meant so much more to me than just,

 a couple in a lonely old town.

To me, it meant hope –

that one day when we look back

we can say that we made it out of

a broken town together as one.

~ Afari

Love is not about being perfect for each other,

it's about two broken people helping each other

heal because in some way we're all broken.

~ Afari

My **thoughts** about you are far vast

than the words I ever utter to you.

~ *Afari*

CLOSER

I sent birds in your direction to sing you lovely

melodies that speak of the love

I have for you, but it rained that day so the birds

couldn't reach you.

I wrote you sweet love letters but the courage to

approach you just wasn't with me.

I stare at you in public but my eyes don't hold the

spark to make you turn around.

I whisper your name with my heart but

your heart is too distant to hear mine call.

I sometimes convince myself to forget about you

But

You're the thirst I cannot quench,

You're the itch I can't scratch away,

You're the butterfly that just won't come my way.

We're the beautiful accident that never happened.

We're the roads that never got to cross paths.

Now, just like time we're looking back at the past

through the eyes of curiosity wondering

what we could have been,

you and I.

~ Afari

THE LITTLE THINGS

The tight hugs,

pinky promises,

awkward conversations,

winks,

goodnight texts,

good morning messages,

kisses on the cheek,

kisses on the forehead,

and the whisper of

"I love you" to the ear.

These are the little things

that mean the most.

I once heard somewhere that "love doesn't keep count"

Yet, here I am endlessly counting the number of times

I fall in love with you each day.

~ Afari

Your beautiful smile is not shaped

by this world yet it shapes my world.

~ Afari

I long for the conversations we never had,

and the kisses we never shared.

I long for everything we never had the chance

to do.

~ Afari

Love says make her cheeks hurt

not by laying your hands on her

but

by making her smile all day.

~ Afari

I'm in constant conflict with love,

I don't know if I'm angry that you broke

my heart,

Or just disappointed that I let you?

~ Afari

Together, we can survive the day and conquer the night. We could dance, hand by hand, side by side under the stars and the day the music begins to fade, then together, we'll dance to the rhythm of our heartbeats.

~ Afari

To love is beautiful but to love

and be loved in return is magical.

~ Afari

Both our hearts had to be broken

for our pieces to fit together perfectly.

~ Afari

Love will endlessly hurt if you constantly

fall for those people that aren't ready to catch you.

~ *Afari*

You're changing and slowly becoming

someone I feel very less in love with.

~ Afari

You are my one reason

to smile **countlessly.**

~ *Afari*

Borrow me your fingers

to fill the empty space

between mine.

~ Afari

Your love gives me the feeling

only a home can give;

the feeling of belonging.

~ *Afari*

When someone finds the path that leads to
your heart they will know that here I where
I have lived.

~ *Afari*

There is unexplainable beauty

that lies in loving yourself.

~ Afari

You are beautiful, I hope you don't

read this thinking it's for every other person

except yourself.

~ Afari

There were are so many things

that changed but the love we

shared was not one of them.

~ Afari

I'm sorry that I could never find the right words to say to you. The words that would let you know that you're beautiful and sadly the kind of words that would make you want to stay.

Perhaps this is why I lost you. I believed that words alone would be enough but it takes so much more than words to keep someone.

~ Afari

It's no longer loving if it feels like hurting.

It's important that you know the difference,

because one day you'll believe that love is

suppose to hurt.

~ Afari

Most women are made of sugar

and spice

but she is no ordinary woman,

her spice was made of glitter and

her sugar was gold.

~ Afari

Tomorrow is never promised so

kiss me today for tomorrow,

kiss me now for a lifetime.

~ Afari

With your lips, you whisper

to my ear saying that you

love me but with your actions

you contradict your words.

~ Afari

To see you smiling brings both

warmth and sadness to my heart.

I'm happy that you're happy yet it

breaks me into a million pieces

because it is not all because of me.

~ Afari

My heart has become a graveyard, and only the word "us"
is engraved on the tombstone.

I still mourn the death of our love, using the memories we
made together as flowers.

~ Afari

You used to be the one reason

that made me smile countlessly but now

you're the reason I'm in countless

kinds of pain.

~ Afari

SIDE BY SIDE

There are many beautiful places in this world that are breath-taking yet out of all these beautiful places my favourite place to be is anywhere and everywhere as long as it's by your side.

~ Afari

It's the way you make me feel that

assures me that your love was worthy

for me to fall for.

~ Afari

Your mistake was believing that

you were the only one between

us that was hurting.

~ *Afari*

Although we both fell in love,

it wasn't from the same height.

We can never be equally broken.

~ Afari

The best conversation is

the one without any words.

It's a silent moment when

all we do is just enjoy each

other's presence.

~ Afari

Right there on your skin, in the places

where you love yourself least is where

I want to plant flowers and water them

with nothing but love and kisses.

~ Afari

At some point in our lives

we desire certain things that

aren't really good for us.

We all have that one thing

that we can't have but crave so badly.

It seems the more we realize we can't

have it the more we want it.

For me, this is you.

~ Afari

YOUR HEART

My home away from home

But now I'm homeless.

~ Afari

YOUR TOUCH

In our lives, we will always have that one person

 that can so easily bring out both the gentleness

and the wildness which is trapped deep within us.

For me that one person is you.

~ Afari

HEARTBEAT MUSIC

As your arms fold gently behind my back, I dearly sink my head into your chest and I listen to the echoes of your heart. I listen to your heartbeat which sings melodies of how tired it is of mistaking other people's arms for home. I wish my ear that lays on you could do much more, like heal you. When I'm in sync with your heartbeat, I fall in love with you. But I always question myself for how such a broken heart can beat so beautifully like music?

~ Afari

If broken crayons can still colour then broken hearts can still beat, and for that they have the potential to still love like they were never once hurt.

~ Afari

She is not like sand that when you hold her,

she slips between your fingers.

No, she is not that kind of woman.

She is more than grains of sand.

~ Afari

I wish I could say that I'm unaffected

by your absence but that would be false.

I miss you, but that does not mean

I am less without you, no.

I'm still me without you, because your presence

does not validate my presence.

I just miss you.

~ Afari

I want us to spend our days getting lost in each other's eyes. Even though we're lost, I know; together we're found in each other's hearts.

~ *Afari*

Your eyes are so beautiful, and they deserve

much more than tears and lonely nights.

Your heart is pure and it deserves more

than empty promises.

~ Afari

There was a time, I found myself staring at ashes. I realised that it's quite difficult to really tell what it was that was burnt. Nobody cares about what was burnt to ashes, I realized that these ashes were my heart.

~ Afari

I wish to be remembered as that person that believed in love even when no one else did.

I want to be the person that still believed in us, even when I had already lost you.

~ Afari

I'M SORRY

I'm sorry I gave you the rainbow when what you wanted was some sunshine. I gave you the sunrise when what you longed for was the sunset.

I'm sorry that I said I love you when you needed me to prove it. I'm sorry for all these things I never gave to you, but don't pretend that what I gave to you wasn't beautiful.

~ Afari

Why do we touch when we can feel?

Why do we like when we can love?

Why do we do less when there is so much for us to do?

Why do we only marvel at the stars

when there is a whole galaxy for us to admire?

~ Afari

When you left for the sunset, I was alone.

I was waiting patiently for the night the

beautiful glow of the stars leads you back home.

Back home to my arms.

~ Afari

ABSENCE

You promised me that you would always be here by my side. You said you would face the world with me. But here I am carrying the weight of the world alone on my shoulders, with only one question spinning in my mind, where are you?

~ Afari

I'm trying to convince a generation that's

deeply wounded that it's still okay to fall in love.

~ Afari

Hold on to what you love for as long as you can because one day it will leave and never return. All you'll have then is just memories.

~ *Afari*

You said that I'm too sensitive but in your night

prayers a gentleman is all that you pray for.

~ *Afari*

You lost her when you failed to see the difference

between "I love you" and "love you".

All because you didn't pay attention is why you

couldn't keep her.

~ Afari

Our love was like a river. Our hearts were like the silent water flowing peacefully between the rocks. Downstream we would flow and just when it seemed like here ends the current, that's when we connected to the ocean.

~ Afari

THE FLOWER THAT STOOD STILL

The sun wanted to burn the flower severely

but it actually made it glow.

The wind wanted to tip the flower over

but actually made it steadier.

The aggressive storm wanted to harm the flower

but in turn made it strong,

and when the rainbow came the became soft once again.

Why do we push away the people that care deeply about us, while we chase people that don't even care about our wellbeing? **People that don't even care about us.** We strive to grab other planets unaware that by doing so we're neglecting the galaxies and stars that are already resting on our palms.

~ Afari

All those that have loved me before said they would love me softly yet they were able to break me into so many pieces. I'm tired of soft love now. I want love that is hard. Love that is hard when I am weak. Love that is hard enough to cover the scars I have like dry cement covers cracks.

~ Afari

We're the seed that never grew

because we failed to water each other.

~ Afari

PAST

It is a very dangerous place to live in.

How saddening it is that the place where

we fell in love is the same place our

love died, and left me in pieces.

~ *Afari*

LADY AFRICA

You are both tender and rough,

Your edges are smooth yet daring.

A true lady of sugar and spice,

is what you are.

I desire to one day restore the hope

that once filled your eyes.

You are dressed in the blood of those

who have tripped before your feet.

You are an unpleasant dream to plenty

but yet and still to me a place that I call

home.

JOY

When the tears fall down your face

only to be met half way by a smile.

That's when you are truly happy.

~ *Afari*

When you told me that your heart isn't a safe

place,

I wish I had whispered "But whose heart is?"

~ Afari

Love does not hide behind shadows,

love embraces the sunlight.

Love brings light to even the darkest

and emptiest of souls.

~ Afari

Although my eyes are filled with tears,

I will try my best not to cry because I know

that this isn't the end and this isn't goodbye.

I know that we'll meet again someday.

~ Afari

FLEW AWAY

You were a little bird when I first saw you. One of your wings were broken, as much as your heart was. I was vulnerable and you were fragile, so I allowed you into my life.

I gave you kindness,
love and respect.

I was good to you.

My heart became your home.
We shared past memories and created some of our own but before I could tell you how I truly feel you had already healed. You were no longer broken. Everything changed as soon as you could swing your Wings once again.

That's when you flew away and left me. My eyes that were once filled with so much compassion for you are now overflowing with tears from you.

I'm not like all the people you've been loving before me.
I am the full-stop to your pain and the start of a new
sentence that begins with love and ends with happiness.

~ Afari

For your heart to grow stronger it had to be broken, so it can know just how much pain it can withstand.

~ Afari

I deserve to be loved, not just with your heart

but with everything that's inside of you.

Love me with your veins,

love me with your skin,

and love me with every inch of your body.

I deserve that kind of love.

~ *Afari*

I'm trapped somewhere between fighting

harder for you, and letting you go.

~ Afari

Every time you look into my eyes I feel both weak and strong. I didn't know what this feeling was or if there was even a name for such a feeling. I feel so empty yet so full.

I had absolutely nothing to give to you, but you didn't want anything from me, besides me. Just me. This feeling was love.

~ Afari

I am a temple of many flaws. I am far off from being perfect but every time you say "I'm yours" it sure feels really close.

~ Afari

You're the blues to my sky,

the stars to my night.

You're the rainbow to my storm,

and the Sunshine to my fog.

~ Afari

How sad it is that the **happiness** we

both search for isn't in each other.

~ *Afari*

The memories I hold so dearly close to my heart are made mostly of people who are no longer part of my life.

~ Afari

You tried to keep me with lies but you couldn't. You knew that you were losing me and when you decided to tell me the truth I was already gone.

~ *Afari*

A GARDEN *of* WORDS

for the mind

DREAMS

When we're older we will discover that

dreams do come true and

our only regret will be that we didn't dream

big enough while we were still young.

~ Afari

STICKS & STONES

I remember a time where we played with sticks and stones. A time where we coloured the sky purple, Trees were red and the Ocean was any colour but blue.

Sometimes I think back to a time when butterflies were chased across fields as the beautiful sunset would fill our eyes and when the night came, do you remember how we use to count the stars?

As time patiently crawled past, we began playing with smartphones. We hardly coloured as much and sadly whenever we did it was in between the lines.

 Nowadays, we hardly play anymore. We pay no attention to the Stars, the Ocean and the Trees. We've become colour-blind, to ever find the beauty that lies in chasing butterflies. Now all we do is only admire as they fly before our eyes.

Today, the only time we look up is when we're in search of a shooting star. Our hands have become too cramped to be out stretched and catch the raindrops falling from the sky. So, all we ever do is sadly watch the raindrops fall and hit against the face of the Earth with no one present to catch them.

A PLACE CALLED HOME

It doesn't matter how many miles

you are away from home, home

will always be close to you.

Home is there on your fingertips,

home is in your heart, and where

ever you may go or which ever

path you choose, home is in you.

~ Afari

CITY LIGHTS

It's in the late hours of yesterday and

The early hours of today that the City is

most alive.

There is something about the City lights

that easily captures your attention.

As the City was beaming with colourful lights,

I realized that the night is more

Beautiful than daytime could ever be.

~ Afari

FORGIVE

Strength is not shown by fighting back
when you're provoked,
true strength is having the courage to
forgive even when not apologized to.

~ Afari

The sting of a Bee only makes

the honey taste sweeter.

~ Afari

BITTER KINDNESS

Regardless of all the bitterness this
world brings forth to the tip of your
tongue,
I hope that you can still recognize the
taste of kindness.

~ Afari

OVERCOMING

"Shoot for the Moon if you fail

you'll land among the stars"

The point is not landing on something but

rather overcoming the fear of failing.

~ Afari

DEATH

Remember that the world is God's garden.

He may dispose the unwanted weeds off to hell

but he also picks the most beautiful

flowers to decorate heaven.

~ Afari

JOURNEY

Life is not always about the destination,

sometimes it's about the journey,

the hurting, the healing, and the loving

but above all else life is about those

we share the journey with.

~ Afari

I CRY

I cry, not for the blind but for those who are blessed with sight but lack vision.

I hail, not for those without hands but for those who are given hands but never lend them to their neighbour.

I weep, not for the deceased but for those walking the Earth yet remain dead deep within.

I sob, not for the audio impaired but for those who are gifted with Ears to hear but don't listen.

I howl, not for the mute but for those who can speak but never speak to uplift others.

I cry, not for the women who are victims of infertility but for the mother that abandons her children.

Whatever is thought by the mind,

Longed for by heart, and

Spoken by the tongue

Shall be made true to the eye.

~ Afari

When a Village helps someone cross the river

it is that person's responsibility to one day

 return and build a bridge for his village.

~ Afari

TIME

Take things step by step because

half a step towards the right direction is much better

than a gigantic leap towards the wrong direction.

~ Afari

IGNORANT

People usually reveal their true colours
at the beginning but we're too ignorant
to the truth.

We should start seeing people for
what they are and not
who we desire them to be.

~ Afari

A tree can only spread its

roots as deep as the soil allows.

~ *Afari*

We all need something to believe in –

A dream or an idea,

because it's the day we stop dreaming

when we start dying.

Death is not when you stop living,

Death is when you stop dreaming.

~ Afari

Happiness is measured with the moments

that bring tears of joy to our eyes.

~ Afari

Only a person that didn't do their best has regrets,

but a person that does their maximum

best no matter what the final result is they

will always find satisfaction in the work.

~ Afari

Lemon trees **grow**

with water not lemonade.

~ *Afari*

It is not because you can be broken that
makes you a weak person.
It is the will to pick up the pieces and mould
yourself back together that means that
you're a strong person.

~ Afari

GREENS

You are just like a tree, so deepen your

roots and stretch your branches and let

the world know that you're there.
Let the world feel your greens.

~ Afari

Let **kindness** be the

light that guides you.

~ Afari

You and only you can decide what

this chapter in your life gets called.

~ Afari

You may not be perfect but

 you are enough.

Maybe not for the whole world

but for someone; for yourself.

~ Afari

WOMEN.

Dear women,

be the tree that bears pleasant fruits,

be a home to the beautiful birds that sing,

be the tree that purifies the taste of the wind,

be deep rooted and have a strong stem for

the whole world will try continuously to shake you.

~ Afari

MEN

Dear men, being a man is not determined by

how many trees you have climbed.

A real man only climbs the tree he has cared for

throughout many seasons.

He only climbs a tree he has watered in summer,

a tree that he swept that leaves of during the fall,

a tree he gave warmth to in winter,

and a tree he has helped bear beautiful fruit.

~ Afari

PATIENCE

This is beautiful but

this is not for me.

Mine is yet to come.

~ Afari

But what is sleep when you're

already living your dreams?

~ Afari

BLESSINGS

In life, it is those people

with seemingly less than

what we have that can

count our blessings the best.

~ Afari

WOULD YOU?

If our thoughts were to hang above

our heads in speech bubbles,

If our words were to become a new

layer of skin that covered our bodies,

would we still be as beautiful?

~ Afari

Have you ever taken the time to notice
how in life it is usually those people that
know us least that are quick to say that
we've changed?

~ Afari

Most opportunities are not by the 'opening of a door'
but by the window you choose to break and enter through.
Create opportunities.

~ Afari

Go live your life to the fullest.

Discover new things.

Spend time alone.

Know the things that make

you the best version of yourself.

Find out what genuinely makes you

happy, and go after it.

~ Afari

A heart full of hate and jealousy

is more harmful than the deadliest poison.

~ Afari

Years have come and gone but you are still here. It may be a new year but it doesn't have to be a 'new' you. Continue to build yourself from where you left off. You are much more than the days that turn into years. Don't let the days you live in define you but define the days that you live in.

~ Afari

DEPENDENT

Why are you so ridiculously dependent on other people for healing, when you can heal yourself? Don't rely on the Sun, when you can be your own sunshine.

~ Afari

It's only those people who can still dream like little kids that grew up.

~ Afari

When you let go of all the things that don't want to stay, you will realize that you have made room for all the beautiful things that have always been there waiting for you to notice them. The kind of things that will be with you for a lifetime.

~ Afari

Growth comes in many forms. There are times where people will see you grow and you will be blind to it. The opposite is true, too. Growth is an inevitable part of life, but more than seeing yourself grow, it should be enough to know that you are growing. Maybe not exponentially but bit by bit.

~ Afari

The world is a difficult place to get around, but no matter how hard your life may be, home should be the easiest place to go back to.

~ *Afari*

No matter how little your light seems to beam,

it still has the potential to bring light to the whole world.

Even the smallest star still brings a glow to the night sky.

~ *Afari*

LET IT BE

There are things in life that should never be forced into existence.

These things ought to unfold to us naturally,

as if it were just another bird flying through the sky or as simple as taking your next breath.

When these things are forced to be, we will never fully appreciate them, at least the way they should be.

These things come with time.

Falling in love and being kind to someone these are the things we should never hesitate to do.

WISER

I remember being afraid of being seen a certain way. I had to be constantly aware of the kind of clothes I wear and the kind of words I choose to say. Now I'm older and I'm much wiser, and one thing I've learnt in my years is that people will always choose what they see in you regardless of what you're trying to show them.

~ Afari

It is not possible to heal if you're still holding on to all the things that continuously hurt you. We can't be free to grow if we don't release ourselves from all the things that keep us prisoner. Let go of all the things that don't allow you to be your true self.

~ Afari

When I was younger I was too naïve to believe that some of the things we hold dear to our hearts are worthless things to other people. I thought that if I love something then surely everyone ought to be in love with it too. I was raised with humbling sayings like "one person's trash is another person's treasure." I knew what this meant but I never thought it would apply to me. I was wrong because the person I love is not resting peacefully in my arms but now that I see things differently I'm beginning to see the depth of this. What is useless to one person is what someone else is praying for. Just like when the heavens cry tears of rain yet the soil calls this an abundant blessing.

~ Afari

REFLECTION

I'm stuck in between choices and decisions to be made.

I'm trying to make decisions that are different from my younger self while also trying to make choices that my future self will one day be thankful for.

~ Afari

Learn to silence the voices that surround

you and for once listen to the one within.

Pay less attention to the hemlock flowers

around and listen to the Sunflower that's inside of you.

~ Afari

Is it possible for an oak tree to grow at the bottom of the ocean? No it is not, however there are plants that grow underneath water. There are plants that require more sunlight, and there are some that need more water than others to survive. What is good for someone else may not be good for you. Be content with where you blossomed and grow from there.

~ Afari

Don't judge the next person, we're all fighting different battles within ourselves. We don't have the same scars and our wounds aren't equal in their depth.

~Afari

It is often our appreciation of

the little

blessings that makes provision

for bigger blessings.

~ Afari

Get hurt once, and never cry away

your tears over the same thing twice.

~ Afari

for the soul

We've become **ghosts** to each other's hearts

But we're still **heroes** in each other's dreams.

~ *Afari*

Life is less about who we'd die for

but rather it's about who we'd

fight the arms of death to spend

more time with.

~ Afari

Tomorrow might mean less of a day to you than it does to me. Through my eyes tomorrow is just another chance for me to see and **admire** the beauty that rests upon every corner of your body.

~ Afari

We have to start raising children that won't count their childhood as one of their **scars.**

~ *Afari*

Not being a Rose doesn't mean you're not sexy,

it just means you're a **different** kind of beautiful.

~ *Afari*

The world has us convinced that

only crazy people talk to themselves

so much that we became terrified to

tell ourselves that **"We are beautiful."**

~ Afari

IN YOUR SHADOW

I've become one with the darkness of your shadow, this not
by choice but by fear of what could be.
Scared of stepping into your light, I choose to love you from
the darkness of your shadow.

As each day passes and as you constantly shine,
I become more of the stranger that falls in love
with you from the dark.

I beg of you to take a closer look at the darkness
of your shadow for a second more and perhaps
you'll notice that someone is gazing back at you smiling.

I choose to love you from the darkness of
your shadow not by choice but because
it's the only way I've ever known how to love.

What happens when fire meets gasoline?

Us.

~ Afari

TOMORROW

If tomorrow never comes, let the water drown me
but allow me to use my last breath to tell you that
I love you.
If tomorrow never comes, let the fire burn against my skin
yet
leave behind imprints of where you last touched me. And
If tomorrow never comes, let the sky take me while
looking into your eyes.
At least I'll die looking at something **beautiful.**

In a world where darkness roams;

You're my light.

In a season filled with rain;

You're my sunshine.

In a place where there's chaos;

You're my peace.

~ Afari

If seeing is believing,

loving is feeling then this

hurting could be my healing.

~ *Afari*

Whenever I look at myself in the mirror,

it feels like I'm just a man standing in the rain

looking into a house repossessed of its furniture.

A house filled with darkness because of

unpaid electricity bills.

A house with broken glass windows.

A house no one wants.

A house that was once a home.

~ Afari

I am a soul unfamiliar with the wonders

of the world but deep within

I know that you are one of them.

~ Afari

You said you want to taste my soul but

my kiss ends with me biting your lips.

Then, you said you want to know my love but

my pleasure is one with the pain.

~ Afari

ROSE

She appears to be weak yet she can bloom

in between the cracks of concrete.

She seems soft

but beware of her thorns.

She withstands the storm with her stem

standing upright.

She is aware of her uniqueness yet

she can be found in the midst of weeds.

Could it possibly be that her triumph over

these battles

is what makes her strong and beautiful

deep within her soul?

IN YOUR ARMS

Home has become more than a building with four walls surrounded by windows and topped off with a roof. But I've found a place to call home in your warm and loving arms.

~ Afari

When you left I couldn't close the door

A part of me always had hope that

you would one day find your way back home.

~ Afari

LIGHT BEAM

It is our brokenness that makes

 provision for happiness.

It is through the cracks that

the inner light within our souls can

beam through.

~ Afari

Don't let the fear of being hurt

stop you from loving whole heartedly

~ *Afari*

Be careful, even

Roses have thorns.

~ Afari

SEEDS THAT GREW

My soul was just a plant-less garden but

you were a gardener.

You planted flower seeds in parts of me

that were long dead.

You used love and kindness to water the seeds

Yet you never stayed long enough to see

those seeds blossom into flowers.

~ Afari

Sometimes I look past the beauty that lies in

your eyes directly to my reflection in your Iris.

I only do this because I hope to see what you

see in someone like me.

~ Afari

A BIT OF YOU

We're now apart, but

there's still a bit of you left in my heart.

I wish the memories would fade like the smoke

of a cigarette, but

there's still a bit of you I can't forget.

I take plenty of wine sips, but

 there's still a bit of you left on my lips.

I've seen sunsets and I know the seashore, but

there's still a bit of you I was yet to explore.

I try to get you out of my head, but

 there's still a bit of you left in bed.

We're both free to be, but

 there's still a bit of you left in me.

CLOSURE.

Don't return to the same arms
that hurt you to find healing.

If those arms couldn't provide
Warmth then they can never provide
Closure.

~ Afari

TOGETHER

You live for the sunrise

I live for the sunset.

You're a singer and I'm a dancer.

You admire the calm waves of the ocean

I adore the view from the mountain's peak.

You belong to spring and

I belong to summer

Yet, here we are

Standing together.

~ Afari

YOUR SMILE.

Your smile is sweet yet your words are bitter,
Your hug is warm yet your hands are cold,
Your heart is close yet your love is so far away.

~ Afari

IN & OUT

What is seen on the outside is

what attracts them

 but what is found within

 is what makes them stay.

~ Afari

Our bodies are stuck at 32

Yet

Our souls are as wild as 18.

~ Afari

FEAR OF LETTING GO.

You ask me,

" Why don't I fall in love?"

"Why am I so afraid of holding on?"

I don't fear holding on,

I'm absolutely terrified that

I'll still be holding on

Even when the time to

Let go comes.

LOST

I often purposefully get lost.
I leave behind a trail of footprints
 for you to find me
but you hardly come looking.

I'm like a book awaiting to be read,
 a song waiting to be sung and
a seed waiting to taste the soil,
 I'm here waiting for you to find me.

And even when I'm lost the
burning desire
 to be only found by you consumes me.

It all hurts because we left some

things unsaid and

some stones unturned.

~ Afari

THE MOON AND STARS.

What if the stars are the scattered pieces of the

Moon's broken heart?

A heart broken into a million pieces to

fill the galaxy,

A heart broken into a million pieces to

fill my eyes with beauty

But

How can such a tragic heart break be

breath-taking?

CARPE DIEM

Hold me a bit longer,

hug me a bit tighter,

kiss me a bit harder,

and look into my eyes a bit deeper

because I won't be here forever.

~ Afari

Love comes in many different forms

But yours was the one that hurt me the most.

~ Afari

US.

For both of us falling in love was never

in the realms of possibility.

You had roses blooming in your heart

while

bullet shells were falling from my mind.

~ Afari

I write about hurting because

that's all you ever made me

feel.

~ Afari

MAYBE

Maybe if I loved you a bit harder,

Maybe if I gave you more flowers,

Maybe if I called you that one night

Maybe, just maybe you'd still be mine.

~ Afari

REJECTION

One day you'll seek for my love.

You'll try to call me

but I will not be there to respond.

Then,

You'll go searching for me in places you used

 to see me but I won't be there.

You'll wait for me to return

but I won't come because I'll be long dead;

killed by your rejection.

And in the depths of my heart your existence

will soon into nothingness disappear,

as I fall into the arms of another.

It's the way you always look deep into my eyes that tells me that I am beautiful. The kind of beauty not even the words you say to me can equal.

~ Afari

He is the dark universe and she is the bright stars.

She brings light into his world and yet

as much as he needs her, she also needs him to shine.

~ Afari

BETWEEN THE LINES

She is not fighting with you when she argues,
she is subtly fighting for you.
It's when she's quiet when you should know
that you're slowly losing her.

~ Afari

I APOLOGIZE

Forgive me for the issues

I've never really learnt how to trust, and

Forgive me for the hurting

I've never really known how to love.

~ Afari

SHE LEFT

She was to me as the waves of the ocean

is to the shoreline.

She came and she went.

She never stuck around much.

Her departure caused a void within my heart.

A void I now use to grow flowers to give to her

When she comes back,

If she comes back,

I hope she comes back.

TO FORGET OR NOT.

I wish I knew how to forget about you, but

even when my eyes are completely

shut you're still all that I see.

We've shared so many memories together sometimes

I wonder if I really can't get myself to forget

about you or is it that I just simply don't want to.

~ Afari

WHEN IT ALL STOPS

When the dust settles and our vision is clear,

we will know who was by our side and who wasn't.

When the earthquake stops and everything is

back in its place, we will know who would strive

to keep us safe and who wouldn't.

When the storm's time is due and the sky is once

again blue, we will know who would stick by us

and who wouldn't.

When the flood is no more and the land is dry

once more, we will know who would risk their

lives to save us and who wouldn't.

When we are free from the famine and we

have food, we will know who would break

bread with us and who wouldn't.

Together we can turn today's

moments into tomorrow's memories.

~ *Afari*

If flowers were to bloom everywhere

you've smiled the world would

be a much more beautiful place.

~ *Afari*

Words that are spoken can often hurt

but it's the words that are left unsaid

that hurt the most.

~ Afari

We promised each other forever

but your definition of forever

was different to mine.

~ Afari

We all hurt and

we all heal differently.

~ Afari

The most beautiful flowers are those

found in the most unexpected places.

~ *Afari*

Tomorrow is never promised

so kiss me today for tomorrow.

~ Afari

When we kiss it feels like

my lips are dreaming.

~ Afari

I can't forget about you because

you're still all that I see in my dreams.

~ Afari

You convinced me that
I was your universe.
With gentle love
and a kiss you turned
my scars into stars.

~ Afari

In the same way that love holds

the curse to hurt us it also

has the power to help us heal.

If love can be the poison then

love itself can be the remedy.

~ Afari

When she saw her mother being hurt by her father,

she was convinced that loves only comes through pain.

Sadly, when he saw his father hurt his mother,

he believed that this was the way to love a woman.

~ Afari

It's our own arms that often

provide the best kind of healing.

~ *Afari*

I want to be filled with so much love, generosity and happiness that it overflows and spills over to fill other people's lives.

~ Afari

It's not every wound that heals perfectly.

There are **wounds** that turn into scars,

 which then become a reminder of how much

we have endured and still survived.

~ Afari

Often when it's time to

say the final **goodbye**

I think of your first hello.

~ *Afari*

Embrace the tears falling from your face

let them roll,

the saltiness is the pain finally letting go

your body is being unburdened,

the cleansing of your soul.

And if the tears are of joy,

the saltiness leaving the

body is making way for happiness.

~ Afari

I need someone

to *unhurt* me.

~ Afari

Love comes in gentle tears of joy

yet the healing comes in salty

tears of brokenness.

~ *Afari*

Always strive to keep the fire within your

spirit burning wildly, although the

flames are within you, they can

still be the **light** that someone

 else depends on.

~ Afari

Right there on your skin,

in the parts you love yourself least

is where I want to pour my love for you.

Right there, is where

I want to plant flowers and

water them with love.

When the seeds grow into flowers

perhaps through them you will learn

how to love yourself once again.

~ Afari

I hate how easy it was for you to let

me and everything we've shared go.

~ Afari

NUMB

Sometimes it feels like I have
forgotten how it feels to feel.

~ Afari

Old Days

I miss those days.
The days we took the
night that was young
to talk about the days that
were old.

~ Afari

More than your lips, find someone

that can kiss your heart and your mind.

Find someone who could kiss

every inch of you.

~ Afari

THIS, SHE IS.

She is the ocean and its waves.

She is the storm and the thunder.

She is the rain as she is the rainbow.

She is a warrior in armour yet a queen in a castle.

She endures and she conquers.

She is gentle in her touch but

her stride awakens the earth.

She is a garden of many and different flowers.

She is the blues of the sky and the

clouds that decorate it.

She is wild.

She is strong.

She is bold.

She is beautiful.

She is a WOMAN.

DANCING ON ICE.

We were like an airplane flying fifty thousand feet but with just one wing to steady us. As a result, we lost our balance. I remember how side by side we used to be, I was the bold and you were the italics. I was told that such things happen when people dance on ice. Dancing on ice, that was us. But now I wonder if the ice that once held us like a young girl holding a butterfly at the end of her fingertips melted, or if it was us that stopped dancing.

~ Afari

DYING AND GROWING WITHIN

Sometimes you look at a plant and see that it is dry as it is dying, but you're just looking at its "face" value. There might be so much more going on within it, which you're unaware of. The plant might be growing silently from within because the world is not ready to carry the kind of fruits it bears.

~ Afari

WARMTH

I asked her 'how is it that single people give the best love advice?' She said "It's because single people have been loving themselves long enough to know their worth and just like the chests that are home to the most broken of hearts can also give the warmest of hugs."

~ Afari

When I thought I lost you, my heart

whispered that you were never even mine.

~ Afari

It wasn't the distance that killed us.

What really killed us was the silence,

the distance was just the poison.

~ Afari

How wonderful it is to live a life of collecting memories and chasing sunsets, while trusting in the stars to lead us back home.

~ Afari

It feels like there is nothing that I could do to help her. It feels like not even my words can reassure her that she is beautiful after the world has made her feel like she isn't.

~ Afari

She is already a queen, but she is still yet to reach her full potential.

~ *Afari*

FIRE WITHIN US

We were like a matchstick being lit.

We were a spark; a flame forged by love.

This was us, a fire fuelled by the

promise of forever.

We grew to become a wild and untameable blaze;

An inferno of precious memories.

We burnt everything in our path like lava;

it all ended in ruins.

This fire of wild flames got

Unstable.

We're now a smoke of memories

slowly fading into nothingness.

The fire that was within us,

burnt everything and sadly

It burnt us as well.

You thought I was someone you can

easily burn through,

But I can never be burnt by you.

The flames of the fire

I contain within me are far greater.

~ Afari

Where ever your feet may take you,

there will always be a sunset close by.

And stars in the sky to fill your eyes.

~ Afari

Sometimes I wish I could taste my own lips,

just to know how good I've been to you.

~ Afari

Some nights I feel closer to the moon,

some nights I wonder where the moon is

and some nights I feel like I am the moon.

~ Afari

I don't just let the good times roll,

I roll with the good times.

I don't live in the moment,

I am the moment.

~ Afari

Say you love me and I'm yours for the moment,

show me your love and forever is ours.

~ Afari

What if the rain that graces the thirsty soil is tears from a sad sky? The water that fall as tears is now a supplement that grows flowers. Nature also hurts but if nature can heal itself then you can too.

~ Afari

To sleep, to dream, a chance to hope.

To stay, to belong, a place called home.

~ *Afari*

It didn't have to be a dream for it to become a nightmare. When you slipped through my fingers like grains of sand, it felt like a tragedy without the presence of death but with the torture of departure.

~ Afari

While the world was expecting a Rose to bloom, she blossomed out as a Sunflower and she was beautiful in her unpredictability.

~ *Afari*

I blossomed in the place they least

expected me to. I grew right underneath their feet.

~ Afari

I look into your eyes and I think to myself, are you my next heart-breaking poem or will you become a reason for me to still believe in love?

~ Afari

It's really sad how the face that carries the lips that smile the most is also home to the eyes that know the most tears.

~ Afari

Nobody could ever tell that she was unhappy. She would smile often but no one knew that she only raised her cheeks higher so she could stop the tears from falling down.

~ Afari

You've come a long way.

You've seen people fall in love and later fall out of it.

You've seen many tears of both sorrow and of joy.

You've seen things begin and things end.

But **you are still here.**

~ Afari

You hold me steady and deep like the ocean

holds the anchor yet together

we are the sunset in the eyes of the sailor.

~ Afari

Don't ever settle for the rotten fruit that lies on the ground when you know that you deserve the fresh fruit which hangs on the tree.

~ Afari

You were never wrong to say how you truly felt. Most people separate because they rarely ever spent time to talk about how they are feeling. Communication is vital in any relationship and even though we went our separate ways I'm proud to say that I was honest about the things I said I feel for you.

~ Afari

Don't be in despair when the sun

burns your leaves.

Let them fall off.

Tomorrow your leaves will be

much stronger than yesterdays'.

~ Afari

We gave each other some space

so we could both breathe.

But, I was in anticipating every

breath we take to lead

us closer to one another.

~ Afari

My younger self wanted someone that would fight for me, now all I need is someone to just whisper to my ear and remind me why I'm fighting. I need someone to remind me that I'm fighting for the right reasons.

~ Afari

I

Want

You

 in

all

the

ways

there

are

 to

want

someone.

~ Afari

THANK YOU FOR READING,

YOU HAVE NOW HEALED.

CONNECT WITH US.

@wordsbyafari

@spiceandboon

Facebook Page: Spice And Boon

Facebook Page: Afari

@SpiceAndBoon

@AfariWrites

Please share videos or pictures of your moments reading "A Garden of Words". Let's connect the world with poetry.

Let the spirit of love, peace and unity continue to reign.

A GARDEN *of* WORDS